Developing A Local Ministry's Sending Strategy

I0159598

Developing A Sending Strategy.
By Ryan Shaw

Published by IGNITE Media

GMMI
100 County Rd. 263
Armstrong, MO 65230
www.globalmmi.net

ISBN: 978-1-956435-09-2

All Scripture quotations are taken from the New King James Version. Copyright 1982, Thomas Nelson,Inc.

Cover Design – Bew Kanokkan Puranawit
Formatting Design - Acts Company, Chiang Mai, Thailand

More copies of this writing can be ordered from www.globalmmi.net or by contacting info@globalmmi.com

Ryan Shaw can be personally contacted at rshaw@globalmmi.net.

Chapter I.

A CALL TO MINISTRY

Local Leaders Guiding Their Fellowships
With Cross-Cultural Mission Vision

Local ministry pastors, pastoral leadership teams, campus ministry leaders and Bible school faculty and leadership possess an essential responsibility before God: inspiring, educating and activating disciples in the Great Commission. We have already seen that the fulfillment of the Great Commission is the primary purpose of the body of Christ. The chief end of local ministry leadership, therefore, according to Ephesians 4:12, is "the equipping of the saints for the work of the ministry, for the edifying of the whole body of Christ."

Through the guidance and equipping of local leaders, churches and campus ministries are equipped to do the work of ministry. It is common to find leaders' and their ministries buying into the view that it is a local ministry leader's role to do the work of the ministry. Instead, spiritual leadership provides a spiritual environment to guide, envision and empower the people of God under their care toward the formation of Christ within every believer and activation in their primary role within the Great Commission. The primary end of spiritual leadership's preaching and teaching of the Word of God is to build up local bodies in spiritual maturity, proceeding toward their destinies among the unreached and unengaged. Therefore, the primary responsibility of local ministry leaders is providing an overall atmosphere for every disciple to be mobilized and equipped for their roles and calling in the Great Commission.

If at first sight these words seem unrealistic, it is only because local churches and campus ministries have generally given a low priority to the Great Commission. We have gotten away from the great truth of Scripture that the body of Christ is ordained and purposed by God to carry His redeeming love to all the world. Jesus was resurrected to free every human being from the shackles of sin and its bondage. God wills that none should perish. The Holy Spirit, emblazing the Church globally, exists that Jesus be exalted and the Father glorified as the Gospel is brought to all unreached and unengaged people groups, with multitudes being born again. One of the Holy Spirit's primary roles is taking sinners, making them disciples, forming Jesus within, conforming to the image of Jesus, equipping with spiritual power and authority, and preparing for their specific role n the Great Commission. Spiritual leaders, therefore, are accountable to God for the "perfecting of the saints for the work of ministering." Local ministries not properly equipping their people will not find themselves useful by the Lord in the Great Harvest.

The secret of enabling local churches and campus ministries to effectively engage with unreached and unengaged people groups globally is one of leadership. Pastors and spiritual leaders play the essential role in guiding local ministries to be envisioned and equipped in the Great Commission. Due to their positions of leadership, they are a mighty force toward the fulfillment of the Great Commission. History reveals the global body of Christ has made its strongest Great Commission headway when local churches and campus ministries, led by leaders ablaze with vision and anointing from the Spirit, are becoming mobilized and equipped.

Spiritual leadership in local churches and campus ministry fellowships is central to God's purpose in the Great Commission. Leaders have been entrusted to inspire, educate and equip disciples in understanding the Great Commission and being activated in their roles in serving it. This is no easy undertaking. It requires a willingness on the part of local leaders to further prepare themselves of their own grasp, vision and passion in the Great Commission. Additionally, a willingness to implement new points of emphasis to see Great Commission vision brought into local ministry settings is needed. This "Handbook for Great Commission Ministries" has been designed to empower local leaders to guide and equip their fellowships with proven means for cultivating Great Commission vision, passion and strategic plans. In this way, local churches and campus fellowships become directly activated in global harvest and the fulfillment of the Great Commission.

I. The Key - Great Commission Ministries

The key to great harvest and the fulfillment of the Great Commission is the awakening and activation of local churches and campus ministry fellowships prioritizing the Great Commission under able spiritual leadership. A local fellowship becomes an "incubator" for the development of Great Commission understanding, vision and passion. They have ongoing cross-cultural mission fervor developing at a grassroots level from within. It is through the whole body of Christ – every disciple in their assigned roles, every local church and campus ministry becoming activated – that we align with God toward great harvest and the fulfillment of the Great Commission in this generation.

For too long, the Church of Jesus Christ globally has relied on a few "professionals" to serve the Great Commission. We have failed to recognize the biblical mandate of all born-again believers being redeemed for participation in a particular role in the Great Commission. Most local churches and fellowships have failed to prioritize the Great Commission because of this false understanding of a few "professional missionaries" taking up its responsibility. To obediently engage with God and His purposes, every local church and campus ministry is responsible to do its part in teaching, equipping and activating believers in its fellowship in the Great Commission. We must repent, which implies a change of course as we proceed onward.

What are primary areas leaders serve disciples under their care towards the Great Commission? Let's consider four:

1. The local leader spiritually equips disciples. Local ministries reproduce disciples according to the depth of spiritual life within the ministry itself. This depth of spiritual life is set by the spiritual leader. Disciples will generally not ascend to higher spiritual heights than what they are being taught or modeled. The local

leader's primary role is to model, teach and reproduce Jesus' standards of discipleship among the local ministry. To see a Great Commission Ministry become what Jesus intends, local leaders teach, preach and model the depths of the Word of God and knowing and walking with Christ. We consider this more in the section of the handbook about "Abandoned Devotion for Jesus!" (See p. 27).

2. The local leader helps educate disciples. This refers to education in the realm of understanding the nature of the Great Commission. This includes intellectual understanding yet also experiencing God's heart for the nations through spiritual discernment and revelation and His plans for restoring them. Such education begins with gaining scriptural clarity on the centrality of the Great Commission in the Word of God. The Spirit inspires us with this central thrust of Scripture. It continues by growing in prayer for unreached and unengaged peoples. It is further developed through information about the current state of the Great Commission and what the Spirit is doing to engage the unreached through His people. The local leaders do not need to do this on their own, however. This handbook has been developed to serve the local leaders in helping educate their own disciples. We consider this further in the section on Implementing Four Core Components for Mobilizing Ministries (See p. 37).

3. The local leader helps recruit/mobilize disciples in their roles. We see that every disciple has a role in the Great Commission. The local leader helps implement tools and teachings that enable disciples within their fellowships to cultivate a heart for the nations and to discern the specific way God has ordained they be involved. See the section on Every Believer Redeemed for the Great Commission – Six Primary Roles (See p. 115) to grasp this concept and help disciples discern their primary roles.

4. The local leader helps develop a sending strategy to the unreached/unengaged. (See p. 103) By the leading of the Spirit, prayer and considering the gifting, calling, spiritual

maturity and preparation of disciples in their fellowship, teams of disciples are identified to relocate to an unreached area. A self-sustaining plan is developed, serving this small community of message bearers with the initial financial help of the local ministry. This process can be done over and over again towards a goal of sending out 10% of disciples from a local ministry to the unreached in message bearer teams.

II. The Crucial Factor of Success

Only spiritually fervent local ministries are able to carry out the spiritual command of Jesus in the Great Commission. This requires, then, that local ministries are seeking the deepest and highest levels of spiritual life possible. The low understanding and spiritual zeal to obey Jesus' command correlates with the low spiritual life of the Church. The great lack of praying, giving, advocating, promoting, sending and going reveals significant needs: (1) the need for a great revival of spiritual life; (2) the need for true and fervent devotion to Jesus; and (3) the need of entire surrender to serving Him.

It is the lack of the above three needs in Christ's Church that directly leads to the neglect of Jesus' command in the Great Commission. The most important emphasis in seeing the fulfillment of the Great Commission in this generation is not focusing on the needs of the world, but in helping to revive the spiritual life of local churches and campus fellowships in order that spiritual fervor for cross-cultural mission might follow.

To see the command of the Great Commission given its rightful place, we make a definite surrender to be filled with the Holy Spirit and the love of Jesus Christ. We cultivate daily, abandoned devotion to Jesus, crowning Him Lord and King over every area of life. Abandoned devotion to Jesus is essential. It is the fountain from which springs growing love, surrender to Christ and His purpose, faith in His abiding power, and a desire to see His followers giving their lives to make Jesus King over all unreached and unengaged people groups. We will consider these issues more in the section of the Handbook entitled Ministries Ablaze with Abandoned Devotion (See p. 27).

III. Overcoming a Negative Stereotype

A negative stereotype about "missions" and the "Great Commission" has been growing over recent years. Local ministries and leaders have an important role in overcoming these false stereotypes. It is the idea that those involved as God's message bearers are cast-offs from local ministries – those who could not make it in other roles in the church. Maybe they are annoying ones the pastoral leadership wants to get rid of. Alongside this wrong conception of true message bearers is the corresponding idea that those involved in mission are assigned to poverty and why would anyone seek out such a life.

Local ministries can reverse the negative stereotypes by coming in the opposite spirit and engaging the "best and the brightest" from our ministries for global harvest. We do not hold them back for leadership roles in the church or campus ministry but joyfully release them for God's purposes in the earth. The "best and the brightest" are the most spiritually astute and qualified, disciples in our ministries who are excelling in following Jesus wholeheartedly and are being used fruitfully in local ministry endeavors. Their lives are surrendered to Jesus and are pursuing the New Testament standards of discipleship. The law of the Kingdom is disciples will only reproduce in others what we are spiritually in ourselves. Jesus deserves individual local ministries sending out the spiritual "best and brightest" to unreached and unengaged people groups.

IV. Great Commission Ministries Empowered by the Spirit

As local leaders align their ministries with Jesus and His Great Commission, it is necessary to rely upon the Person of the Holy Spirit. We live in a day where technique, organizational machinery and various methods are at a premium. What the body of Christ needs more than ever is a return to the New Testament standard of abiding in the presence of the Spirit of God. We tend to spend more time in committees and strategy meetings than in wholehearted prayer before the living God. We need a fresh return to the power dynamics Jesus Himself promised in connection with His Great

Commission. We hunger for a fresh baptism of spiritual fire and power to faithfully obey His commands, producing eternal fruit among the unreached and unengaged.

God gives the gift of spiritual power as we engage with Him through persevering prayer. The two concepts of spiritual power and prayer are linked throughout the New Testament. Since the upper room prayer meeting prior to Pentecost, prayer has been the secret of spiritual power, perseverance and victory in the face of great challenges and difficulties. The great message bearers throughout history, including the apostle Paul, possessed first and foremost great prayer lives. Prayer was the great work of Paul during every crisis and challenge in his missionary journeys. He believed in the power of prayer and saw tangible answers that produced greater confidence in God and in prayer. Prayer was more to Paul than merely a means to answers. It was the primary means of developing wholehearted devotion to Jesus. He diligently modeled prayer for the churches and believers as the key means of seeing spiritual maturity cultivated within them. Throughout his epistles, we find his "apostolic prayers" for believers. These powerful prayers full of insight and spiritual revelation are crucial in praying for our local ministries and the body of Christ as a whole to become all that God has spiritually ordained them to be.

The early Church in the book of Acts is portrayed as a living fellowship functioning as a dwelling place of God Most High and motivated in all activity by the presence of the Holy Spirit. Global harvest and the fulfillment of the Great Commission is such an impossible task, full of constant challenges, obstacles and opposition, that we must rely upon His supernatural power alone to press forward. It is common to minimize reliance on the Holy Spirit in favor of trusting ideas, human strength, capacities, abilities, infrastructures and human will in pressing forward in God's work. This is not God's way. The Great Harvest will only be reaped through a global body surrendered to the empowering of the Holy Spirit. Let us turn from our ease in trusting in the arm of the flesh and humbly receive more of the Holy Spirit's enabling and empowering by emptying ourselves of all that hinders His divine flow in us and through us.

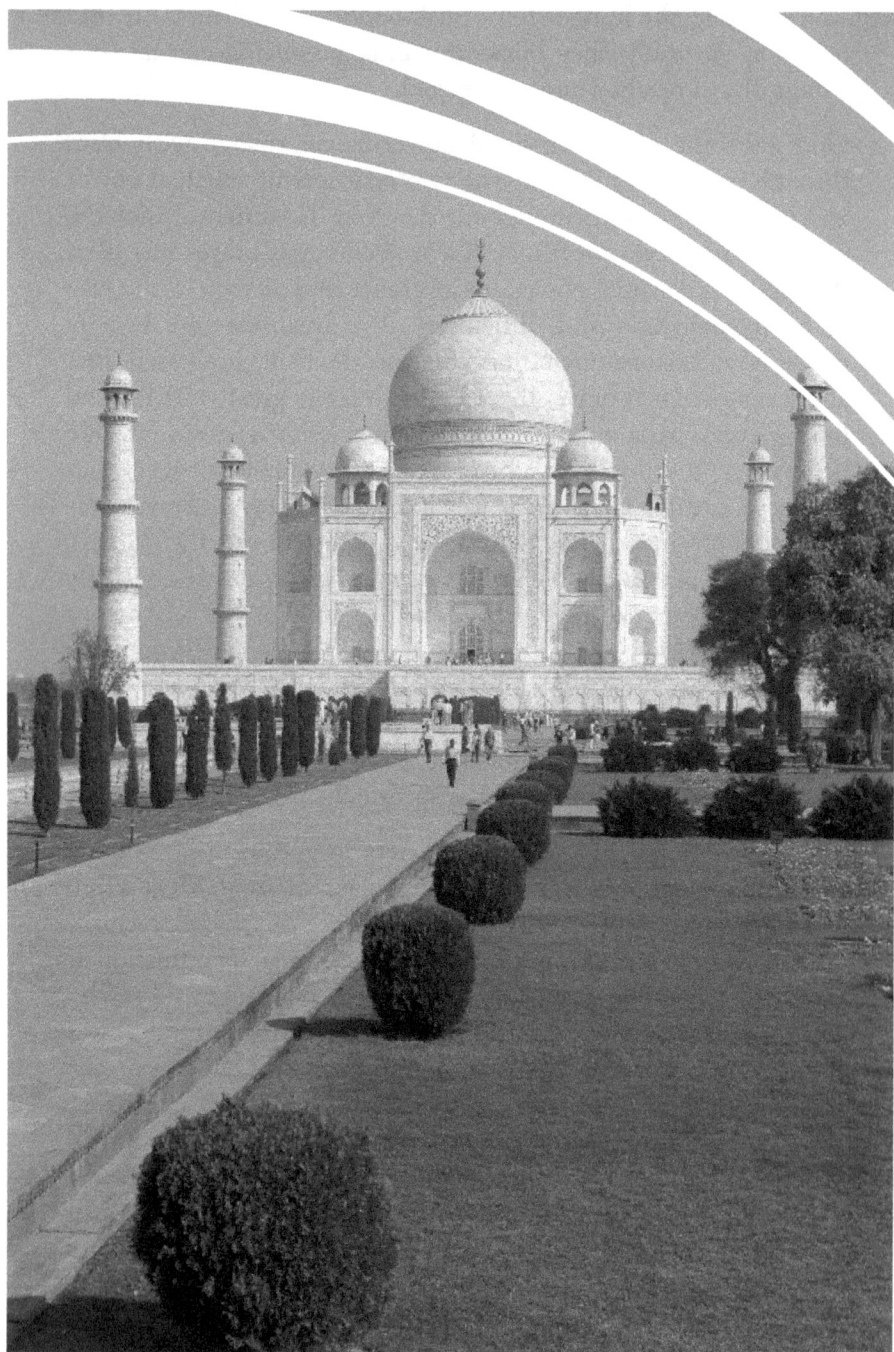

Chapter II.

CREATING A SENDING

Your Great Commission Ministry is well on its way to playing a significant role in the fulfillment of the Great Commission. Your local ministry is presently seeking to cultivate "Abandoned Devotion for Jesus" and raising the spiritual vibrancy and wholeheartedness among the fellowship. It is also implementing the Four Core Components for Mobilizing Ministries and seeing changes in mindset, understanding and activation in disciple's roles in the Great Commission. Fruit is starting to be discerned, and the hearts of many of your members are being aligned with Jesus' vision for the Great Commission.

Next, let us consider how your local ministry can begin to develop a strategy for sending those who are called by God as Message Bearers from your fellowship to the unreached and unengaged.

I. Biblical Foundation for Sending Teams

First, we want to establish the biblical foundation of any local ministry sending out its own disciples as a "Message Bearer Team" to the unreached. Maybe your local ministry is associated with a larger denomination, church network or organization with its own cross-cultural mission department. If this is the case, you are encouraged to discuss the proposed sending strategy with them.

Maybe your local ministry is not connected to any such "cross-cultural missions department." Does this mean you cannot send out your own teams of workers? Of course not! There are many indigenous mission-sending agencies that are available to help and counsel you as your local ministry prayerfully engages with how to send teams of Message Bearers to the unreached. Such organizations and agencies specialize in serving in this way and have learned many of the lessons you will want to learn.

Scripture supports the idea of local churches facilitating the formation and sending of Message Bearer Teams. In the early Church in the book of Acts, God led the formation of the missionary team of Paul and Barnabas that empowered the existing church to develop church planting movements into unreached areas. This is a New Testament model of "Message Bearer Teams" being sent. This sending enables the local churches to participate directly with cross-cultural mission beyond their own geographical areas, specifically pushing beyond where the Gospel is already at work.

A local church engaging this model of sending Message Bearer Teams releases disciples specially called and gifted in this capacity. Through hands on discipleship and leadership development within the local ministry setting, ministry leaders are able to discern those whom the Holy Spirit is calling and appointing in this way. The local sending ministry then is engaged with ministry directly connected to the unreached through these teams while simultaneously being freed to focus on internal and local outreach efforts back home.

II. The Acts 13 Model

Let's take a closer look at how the Antioch Church in Acts 13 reveals a model for forming and sending Message Bearer Teams from local ministries. This chapter of Acts is the beginning of what some might call "intentional mission" in the book of Acts. Mission had been taking place earlier in the book through God leading individuals to various locations (Philip and others) and through scattering the believers through persecution. However, Acts 13 is where the Holy Spirit begins to direct His Church to send out laborers into the unreached harvest.

The Antioch Church would have been a number of individual "house churches" in the city that collectively made up the Antioch Church. It was a multicultural local church with gifted leaders. The Holy Spirit spoke to the leaders during a prayer meeting to separate Paul and Barnabas for the work of going to the unreached with the Gospel. Both of these men were used to help establish the Antioch Church, yet their gifting and calling was beyond the local church. The other leaders of the Antioch Church recognized God's leading and blessed His plans related to them.

III. Guarding Against Unnecessary Control

Some important applications can be seen here. First, the Holy Spirit is the One initiating and directing the process of sending. The Antioch Church released its key leaders in obedience to the Holy Spirit and did not seek to "control" where they would go and how they would do their work. Second, the Antioch Church did not seek to hold back two of its core leaders for local ministry when God had clearly called them to go to the unreached. The church revealed a sacrificial obedience in releasing some of its most gifted leadership to go out. There was a ready release of Paul and Barnabas for the work of church planting movements among the unreached. This is how we are to see local ministries facilitating Message Bearer Teams today. Some who are called are our most gifted leaders, and the temptation is great to selfishly hold them back for our home ministries.

The Message Bearer Team of Paul, Barnabas and John Mark started their church planting ministry. They traveled to Cyprus, Attalia, Pisidia, Iconium, Lystra and Derbe (all in Asia Minor, or modern-day Turkey) planting house churches along the way. Following this, the Message Bearer Team returned to their home base of Antioch to report what God had been doing. This "accountability" relationally linked the new churches being established with the sending ministry. This allowed the sending ministry to more adequately pray for them and understand the new churches' needs.

It is important to point out that the Antioch Church does not appear to have dictated to Paul and Barnabas how to do their work. The members of the Message Bearer Team decided where to go, how long they would remain, who to send to strengthen the churches planted, and how to financially support themselves. All such decisions were made under the guidance of the Holy Spirit. This is important because a sense of control by "sending ministries" can often hinder and even stifle obedience to the Spirit. This is not to say the Message Bearer Team was not accountable to these churches. They most certainly were. But the accountability was not of the dictating type and more of the reporting and encouraging type.

Accountability of the new churches also was not taken up by the "sending ministry" at Antioch but by Paul as he instructed through teaching and letters, providing discipline when necessary, encouraging the disciples, and providing mutual accountability of their leaders. Paul sought to always involve the new churches in the work of mission to the unreached. In doing so, he not only was a pioneer church planter himself but enabled others to be propelled outward themselves.

IV. Church Planting Is Not Denominational Reproduction

Nor was the Antioch Church in any way seeking for Paul and Barnabas to establish new churches that were reproductions of the Antioch Church. The new churches were among people different culturally than those at Antioch, and the Holy Spirit enabled and empowered Paul and Barnabas to plant simple, culturally relevant churches.

Here, too, some applications are clearly seen. Because facilitating church planting movements among the unreached requires obeying the Holy Spirit and considering the culture of the people to be reached, it is not likely that the churches planted will look anything like the "sending church" back home. They are in a completely different situation and cultural context and should not look the same in form and structure. It is not uncommon for denominations or organizations to "control" the teams they send out and seek to reproduce their brand of denominational church wherever they go. This has created great problems throughout mission history and is something to be cautioned against.

V. What Is A Church?

In order to effectively possess a heart-level burden and vision for church planting movements (CPM's) we first need to be clear on what a local church is and what it is not. In the book of Acts, local churches are seen to be the means and even the goal of outreach. Jesus' commission in Matthew 28 calls us to make disciples and it is implied that disciples are gathered together in small communities of faith. These new communities of faith had biblically defined functions and leadership roles but very few defined forms and structures. This seems to be purposefully left out by the Holy Spirit in order to allow for flexibility in each particular situation being faced. It is the same today. We want to be careful not to implement culturally defined ways of doing church (from our home cultures) among a culture where these forms are meaningless (and even potentially harmful).

At its very core, the Bible advocates a church as being in the local community, contextual to the culture of the local people, self-supporting financially, self-replicating, self-governing, relational, accountable and Great Commission focused. Biblical churches are effectively making disciples, who make disciples, who make disciples.

New Testament churches were generally small (sometimes meeting in homes, sometimes in a small room in the Temple, in the workplaces, etc). They were part of a larger body of believers across their city that made up "the Church." They would periodically (some monthly, some weekly) gather together as a larger entity in the city for the sake of unified teaching and worship. But the bulk of their life and ministry took place within the smaller group. These churches could easily reproduce and they did so quite often.

What are biblical operations of a local church? No matter what culture or what location in the world, the below four criteria are meant to be happening within thriving and biblical churches. Without these four we don't have a church. They are where we want to start as we envision what a church is and what it needs to include among the unreached.

Acts 2:42 lists out four crucial components of a "church." "And they continued steadfastly in the apostles' doctrine and fellowship, in the breaking of bread, and in prayers." Let's look a bit further at these four:

1. Apostles Doctrine –This referred to deep teaching full of spiritual authority and applied directly in the lives of disciples. It was the powerful apostolic teaching and message that God had entrusted to the early apostles. It does not mean the

apostles themselves were the only ones preaching and teaching this message. Under the leading of the Spirit they appointed bishops and elders of small, house church, type churches. These leaders then were responsible for deep, Spirit-empowered, transformational teaching and preaching revealing the ways of God, the beauty of God, the perfections of God, the glories of God, the practical life of a disciple and much more. It was all based on the "apostolic" faith that Jesus had given through the Holy Spirit to Paul and the other apostles and that the New Testament is deeply rooted in. We do well to periodically evaluate ourselves and our teaching and faith to see if we have strayed from the "apostles doctrine" which was entrusted to the early church.

2. Fellowship – It is common to reduce fellowship to meeting together and hanging out. This is a far cry from what the early church understood "fellowship" to be. Fellowship was the life on life depth of relationships that included vulnerability, accountability and deeply getting into each other's lives. It meant deliberately opening oneself to others who did the same to you. This is how we grow and how we experience authentic relationships. God has created us as relational beings who experience the depth of life of God in and through human relationships mean to sharpen us as we willingly allow people in. Apart from true "fellowship," true discipleship is impossible.

3. Breaking of Bread – There is some debate about what is being referred to here. Is it the Lord's Supper of communion or is it enjoying meals together. The context of this verse seems to indicate it is the former. Because enjoying meals together has an element of "fellowship" implied with it and because that item was just listed, it seems likely it doesn't refer to this. In addition, four verses later it specifies how the early church ate meals house to house. There would have been no need to specify this had the author intended this in "breaking of bread." It seems to refer to the critical practice of consistently identifying with Jesus' death and resurrection through communion. Churches are to do this, whether in a formal way or not, doesn't seem to be the emphasis.

4. Prayers – The early church was a praying church. They prayed without ceasing – engaging with the Holy Spirit through a vibrant prayer life. The source of its consistent spiritual power and authority came through the release of prayer and intercession. These prayers do not refer to an opening prayer before a church service or a closing prayer, etc. It refers to a lifestyle of continuous prayer that characterized it.

The church relied upon the powerful presence of God and knew the way to activate it was through powerful prayer. Prayer is the mean of growing in love, humility, death to self and much more. Prayer is the means God uses to bring His power down and bring forth His Kingdom purposes.

Apart from a local body of believers actively and purposefully participating in all four of these activities, Scripture reveals we are not being faithful as a church. No matter what our liturgy is like, our structures, the masses that gather to our building on Sundays, etc. If we are not purposefully being faithful to these four areas, we are not functioning as a true church according to Jesus.

Many non-essential elements have been included over time to our churches. These may be helpful in our home churches yet need to evaluated to see if they are culturally appropriate forms for local churches being planted in a very different culture. These may include the use of buildings, paid clergy, sound systems, certain expectations of dress, the day the church meets and much more.

Jesus says, "where two or more are gathered, there I am in the midst of them!" If these two are engaging in the four criteria above of churches referred to in the book of Acts, and are becoming a dwelling place of the presence of God, then these could technically be a church. Among many unreached people groups, churches need to be mobile, easily able to be hidden (to withstand persecution). They can meet in a factory, under a tree, in an office building or anywhere else believers find themselves.

Such churches are centered thoroughly in Jesus Christ as their head, empowered by the Holy Spirit, motivated by love for God, His body and the world around them, growing (spiritually, numerically, geographically) and are spiritually dynamic and active.

With the model of "releasing" Message Bearer Teams compelled by the Spirit of God to see church planting movements establishing simple local churches among the unreached, spiritual function is maintained but structure and other elements are not prioritized. This is what allows the body of Christ to faithfully push beyond the confines of where churches are currently established. These Message Bearer Teams are crucial as channels of the Holy Spirit to carry the Gospel where it currently is not and see culturally relevant spiritual communities of faith developed. They should not be "controlled" by home local ministries but empowered and provided mutual help when necessary.

VI. Understanding the Basics of Church Planting Movements (CPM's)

Now that we've seen a bit of what a biblical church is, let's consider what "church planting movements" (CPM's) are.

Let's start by considering an astounding verse in Acts 19.

8 And he went into the synagogue and spoke boldly for three months, reasoning and persuading concerning the things of the kingdom of God. 9 But when some were hardened and did not believe, but spoke evil of the Way before the multitude, he departed from them and withdrew the disciples, reasoning daily in the school of Tyrannus. 10 And this continued for two years, so that all who dwelt in Asia heard the word of the Lord Jesus, both Jews and Greeks. Acts 19:8-10

How could the powerful, culturally relevant gospel of the Kingdom have gone out to all of Asia (modern Turkey, Greece, Syria, Israel and Palestine) in two short years? Most believers assume Paul himself went out preaching. We are taught that Paul, the incredible message bearer, singlehandedly went to all these places and saw churches planted. Scripture, however, doesn't reflect this sentiment at all. Instead, we know from the epistles that several of these churches (house church fellowships) were never visited by Paul.

The Gospel went forth so fast with so many small and reproducing churches being developed because of church planting teams. During a three year period that Paul lived in Ephesus he set up a church planting training school in a building owned by a wealthy disciple named Tyrannus. This training program had the specific end in mind of planting rapidly reproducing churches accelerated the process of reaching all Asia with the Gospel in just two short years. Astounding!

To understand how this was made possible we need to get out of our traditional way of understanding "church." Much of our modern understanding of "church" limits our ability to cooperate with this powerful strategy on the heart of God. Some have said our modern model of "church" is the greatest stumbling block to the fulfillment of the Great Commission. We tend to think of a building, paid pastors and leaders, a group of 100 or more, one meeting a week on Sundays and other traditional ideas of "church." The New Testament presents an entirely different approach altogether.

A Church Planting Movement (CPM) is a rapid reproduction of culturally relevant, simple indigenous churches which reproduce themselves within a people group or population segment over and over again. These happen among unreached and unengaged people groups. In other words, they are disciple making movements where obedient disciples make obedient disciples and reproducing churches make reproducing churches. A key concept of CPM's is they develop through multiplication, not incrementally.

A CPM does not add a few churches each year in an area. They multiply exponentially. One church becomes two, two churches become four, etc. Other names bearing the same basic concept as Church Planting Movements are Disciple Making Movements (DMM) and Training For Trainers (T4T) CPM's are indigenous. The Gospel always penetrates a people group through an outside voice (the message bearer). Yet, through deliberate effort on the part of the message bearer and team, the Gospel initiative is quickly transferred to emerging indigenous leadership within the people group. A successful CPM has indigenous believers arising with the same heart of rapid reproduction as the Message Bearer Team possesses. CPM's make Jesus known, transform lives, relationships and communities.

CPM's begin with the idea of a movement. A Message Bearer Team is not working to see one church established, but hundreds and maybe thousands of churches. It is important to get out of the mindset of going to plant just one church and align with the paradigm of seeking a movement of exponentially reproducing small churches. If you plan to plant one church, that is all you will get. If you plan and work toward 100 churches, you will move toward this.

VII. A General Development of a Church Planting Movement

A general development of a CPM will usually include the following steps. This list is not exhaustive and the process is not necessarily as neat as this listing may indicate. There is no "right" speed at which to see these items accomplished. Sometimes, the ground is more ready than others. In certain circumstances the process may happen faster. Don't be concerned with time but with faithfulness and perseverance. In most effective CPM's these characteristics are the primary building blocks that are involved.

1. CPM's start and are sustained in prayer.

2. The Message Bearer Team discern a felt need in the community and directly engage in the community.

3. The Message Bearer Team begins with intentional church planting, not only evangelism by gathering new believers into small communities of faith.

4. The Message Bearer Team participates in abundant sowing of the Gospel through culturally appropriate means within the people group.

5. The Message Bearer Team seek a "person(s) of peace" – a key figure in the community who shows a real hunger for spiritual issues.

6. The Person(s) of Peace (through the coaching and mentoring of the Message Bearer Team) sets up an initial "Discovery Bible Study" (DBS's will be discussed further below) for close network of friends, family members, etc.

7. As some who participated in the Discovery Bible Study come to faith in Jesus they continue to operate together, evolving (over time) into a home fellowship or church.

8. Shared leadership emerges among the indigenous believers (as the key leaders are taught by the Message Bearer Team)

9. Over time the Message Bearer Team will rarely be seen by the non-leadership indigenous believers. They will teach, disciple and pour into the Person(s) of Peace and then expect them in turn to teach the other new believers and not yet believers what they have been taught. It is the 2 Timothy 2:2 principle at work. "And the things that you have heard from me among many witnesses, commit these to faithful men who will be able to teach others also."

10. New believers are taught in a focused manner how to follow Jesus. They are referred immediately to their heavenly Father in prayer (not encouraged to overly look to the Message Bearer Team); they are baptized in water; they are taught to read the Word and journal for themselves asking: A) What does it say? B) What does it mean? C) How can I apply it to my life? (obey it). It is imperative to direct them consistently to foundational passages to their faith and new lifestyle: A) Romans 3-8 (our foundation in Christ) B) Sermon on the Mount - Matthew 5-7 (The Discipleship Lifestyle of the Kingdom of God). They are released to begin sharing their testimony within their own sphere of influence.

11. These new fellowships look for other Person(s) of Peace in their networks who will host other Discovery Bible Study groups. These in time also evolve into home fellowships in a multiplying manner.

VIII. Discovery Bible Studies

A crucial tool has emerged in CPM's being developed – the Discovery Bible Study (DBS). The Discovery Bible Study method is unique. There is no lesson to prepare, nor specific text questions. The Discovery Bible Study is best done in a group of three or more. The goal of the Discovery Bible Study is not to conduct a one-way Bible lesson, but instead to show participants how they can learn from and make sense of Scripture and to introduce them to different Christian disciplines, such as worship, prayer, community, service, and accountability. This makes DBS a powerful tool for cross-cultural evangelism toward the goal of gathering new believers together in small churches and eventually multiplying into a CPM. Because content is driven by questions and conversation, there is no limit to the depth of learning and application a group can experience.

Becoming a disciple of Christ is not a theoretical or academic notion, but a life of relationship with God. It's not about performing or doing anything to earn God's acceptance of me. But because it is a relationship I want to do what pleases Him. I pursue Him motivated by love. He woos and wins me to say, "Yes, by your grace I want to do what pleases you!" Becoming a disciple is all dependent on grace and yet I do need to play my part. Therefore, I need to not only learn what Jesus taught, but to live it out and apply it meaningfully and beneficially in my daily existence. What we do with what we learn is vitally important. This is one of the great benefits of the DBS model.

The primary idea behind DBS is that Scriptural information or revelation plus my commitment to apply the truth of what I've learned into my life will equal my transformation into a disciple of Christ.

Any passage of Scripture can be studied in a group using the DBS model. The following steps are involved in every DBS meeting:

1. Praise and Worship – Ask each person to share something they are thankful for this week

2. Personal Prayer – Ask each person to share what problems they have had this week and pray for each other

3. Ministry and Service – Is there any way the group can help with the above problems

4. Read the Chosen Scripture Passage for the Meeting

5. Ask the Discovery Questions:

    a. What Happens in this passage?

    b. What does this passage tell us about God?

    c. What does this passage tell us about people?

6. Ask the Obedience Questions:

    a. How does this passage change how we see God?

    b. How does this passage change how we treat others?

    c. How does this passage change how we live?

    d. What other questions do we have about this passage?

7. Ask the Share Questions:

    a. Who can you share this story with?

    b. Do you know anyone who needs help? How can this group help them?

Among non-literate cultures, the process would be slightly different. Non-literate cultures are not only those who cannot read but those who can read yet learn better through listening then reading. Many cultures around the world fall into this category. They can read but grasp information better through having the information brought to them in story or oral form. In this scenario of the DBS the only difference is the passage isn't simply read but told as a story. This means that the persona giving the passage needs to know it and its details very well. They communicate the passage to the group in a storytelling format instead of reading it straight from the Bible.

IX. From Creation to Christ Discovery Bible Study

The following Bible passages make up a Discovery Bible Study called "From Creation To Christ." This is a very helpful series of passages leading unbelievers from a host of religious backgrounds through the crucial passages of understanding God as the center of all history, humanity falling into sin and the plan of God to restore lost and sinful humanity from the power of sin and death through sending His Son. The last passage brings them to a choice of making Jesus Lord and savior. Each passage is considered as an individual Discovery Bible Study session using the questions above.

- » Genesis 1:1-25 The Creation Story: God Created the World

- » Genesis 2:4-24 The Creation Story: The Creation of Man

- » Genesis 3:1-13 The Fall: The First Sin and Judgment

- » Genesis 3:14-24 The Fall: Judgment of a Sinful World

- » Genesis 6:1-9:17 The Fall: The Flood

- » Genesis 12:1-8, 15:1-6 Redemption: God's Promise to Abram

- » Genesis 22:1-19 Redemption: Abraham offers Isaac as a Sacrifice

- » Exodus 12:1-28 Redemption: The Promise of Passover

- » Exodus 20:1-21 Redemption: The Ten Commandments

- » Leviticus 4:1-35 Redemption: The Sacrificial System

- » Isaiah 53 Redemption: Isaiah Foreshadows the Coming Promise

- » Luke 1:26-38, 2:1-20 Redemption: The Birth of Jesus

- » Matthew 3; John 1:29-34 Redemption: Jesus is Baptized

- » Matthew 4:1-11 Redemption: The Temptation of Christ

- » John 3:1-21 Redemption: Jesus and Nicodemus

- » John 4:1-26, 39-42 Redemption: Jesus and the Woman at the Well

- » Luke 5:17-26 Redemption: Jesus Forgives and Heals

- » Mark 4:35-41 Redemption: Jesus Calms the Storm

- » Mark 5:1-20 Redemption: Jesus Casts Out Evil Spirits

- » John 11:1-44 Redemption: Jesus Raises Lazarus from the Dead

- » Matthew 26:26-30 Redemption: The First Lord's Supper

- » John 18:1-19:16 Redemption: Jesus is Betrayed and Condemned

- » Luke 23:32-56 Redemption: Jesus is Crucified

- » Luke 24:1-35 Redemption: Jesus Conquers Death

- » Luke 24:36-53 Redemption: Jesus Appears and Ascends

- » John 3:1-21 Redemption: We Have a Choice

X. Further Church Planting Movement Resources

The following are helpful websites providing more insight, ideas and considerations related to Church Planting Movements:

- » Church Planting Movements Booklet by David Garrison - http://www.simplechurchathome.com/PDF&PowerPoint/ChurchPlantingMovements.pdf

- » http://t4tonline.org/

- » http://www.churchplantingmovements.com/

- » http://www.cityteam.org/dmm/about/index.php

- » https://www.youtube.com/watch?v=cmqenWEVPuo

- » http://www.missionfrontiers.org/issue/article/disciple-making-movements-among-unreached-muslims

The following three books are helpful resources to go deeper in this concept of Church Planting Movements.

- » Contagious Disciple Making – Paul and David Watson

- » What Jesus Started: Joining the Movement, Changing the World – Steve Addison

- » Church Planting Movements: How God Is Redeeming a Lost World – David Garrison

Chapter III.

A STAGE-BY-STAGE PROCESS FOR TEAMS BEING MOBILIZED AND EQUIPPED

Your local ministry possesses a biblical and Spirit-led calling to release Message Bearer Teams to the unreached and unengaged. How does God mobilize and equip individuals and Message Bearer Teams within a local ministry? It will usually look something like this stage-by-stage development:

1. An initial desire to go deep in abandoned devotion to Jesus through ongoing discipleship through the local ministry along with an initial filling of the Holy Spirit.

2. Love for Jesus growing in a believer, bringing a total life surrender to obey Him and a growing alignment with God's will in and through their life.

3. A stirring by the Spirit that the person is being called to leadership/ministry and a subsequent commitment in the heart of the individual being made (though they usually do not know the sphere or specifics of that work then).

4. The believer is having their ministry gifts developed within the local ministry under the guidance and leadership of mentors (teaching, evangelism, prayer, healing, discipling others, administration, etc)

5. A person experiencing general cross-cultural mission awareness through conferences, seminars, teachings, Mission Forums, etc and their heart being initially awakened to God's passion for the nations.

6. The individual having their initial excitement deepened through participating in a "Great Commission Bible Study" and "Global Prayer Team" more "Mission Forums" and many times hearing the "Go Declaration" challenge to serve as God's Message Bearer among the unreached. Each time they are more considering if God is calling them in this way.

7. A believer having opportunities locally to search out, befriend, reach out and serve unreached people groups who are living or visiting their city. The best way to learn about other cultures is to find them right around you. We need to be ministering at home first.

8. The individual mobilizing other believers within their own local ministry and beyond to be inspired, educated and activated in the Great Commission, possibly leading Great Commission Bible Studies, Global Prayer Teams, etc

9. Sensing the leading of the Spirit to make a firm commitment to the GO Declaration and for the individual to offer themselves to the Lord and to the local ministry leadership as an eventual message bearer among the unreached.

10. Intentional continual growth in the depths of spiritual life, spiritual disciplines and spiritual equipping necessary to thrive as a message bearer among the unreached.

11. Listening to the Spirit for a geographic area/people group where He may be leading. Allowing God to confirm this through whatever means He chooses.

12. The individual learning everything they can about that area and people group (their culture, language, religious understanding, day to day life, needs, etc).

13. Find people living in their city who might be from this background. Befriending them, learning about life in this place, etc. Ministering to people from the area or people group in the home city before going to the actual area and people group.

14. The individual and local ministry leadership considering if there is an indigenous sending agency (or denominational sending structure) the local ministry and Message Bearer Team can partner with to provide specialty counsel.

15. The individual and Message Bearer Team considering the gifts, professions and skills on the Team and prayerfully discerning how the Team will together sustain themselves financially among the unreached

16. The individual and Message Bearer Team considering the platform(s) the Spirit may have them undertake in the new area and among the new people for the sake of identity as well as financial sustenance.

17. The Message Bearer Team together participating in a thorough church planting movement training course to learn the basic processes of developing church planting movements in the area they will go.

18. The Message Bearer Team participating in trust and other team building exercises together. Developing a team culture (before going out) of mutual love and respect through healthy communication skills, problem solving and conflict resolution.

19. Together, the Message Bearer Team is commissioned by the local ministry and travels to its pre-determined location and people group to commence intense cultural and language learning.

I. Mobilize Teams, Not Individuals

It is important to move away from the idea of recruiting one Message Bearer at a time to become activated in the Great Commission. This is a very individualistic approach, and the New Testament and the heart of God reveal a more communal approach.

The account of Acts 8:1 and 8:4 reveal a persecution against the believers that arose and "scattered" them out to surrounding, unreached areas. As they were scattered, "they went everywhere preaching the Word." They relocated their families, their jobs and their communities to other towns, villages and cities with the express purpose of extending the Gospel. Though we are not necessarily responding to persecution, the phenomenon of what took place is a model for Message Bearer Teams. They willingly "scatter" themselves, their families, their jobs, and their communities to unreached locations where the Holy Spirit guides them.

II. Commitment to Sustainability

The Message Bearer Team lives in sustained community (as the early Church did), looking out for one another. Each member of the Message Bearer Team has a role in the sustainability of the team while also doing ministry. The idea of a local church financially supporting a Message Bearer indefinitely is not in the New Testament. Instead, the model is one of self-sustainability through jobs, professions, agriculture, etc. Paul, Priscilla and Aquila were all church planters who also made tents. This was their means of sustenance. Self-sustaining communities also were the mission sending model of the Moravians as they went about church planting in the 1700s.

Switching our mindset to such a model overcomes the barrier of the "sending church" being unable to send Message Bearer Teams due to perceived poverty. The early Church was overall quite poor yet was used by God to thrust the Gospel out of its initial borders to the unreached. A great stumbling block in the global body of Christ at present is its view of finance in the Great Commission. The Bible never advocates that perceived poverty excuses a local ministry from active involvement in sending Message Bearer Teams to the unreached. God has set up means to supply for His laborers. One major way this is done is through the ongoing work of our hands while serving among the unreached.

Another needed mindset shift enabling financial sustainability is a departure from the idea of a Message Bearer being in "full-time ministry." It is sometimes understood that unless workers have detached themselves completely from all natural means of financial sustenance and doing ministry full-time, they are not as spiritual as the person who is. This is not a biblical teaching. Paul, the greatest Message Bearer ever to live, was not in "full-time ministry," according to this definition. He had a job that supplied for his needs. Was he a spiritual person? Of course! This wrong outlook has often hindered Message Bearers from embracing the God-ordained means of sustenance and harmed themselves, their families and even the work of God in untold ways.

III. A Strategy for Sending Message Bearer Teams

What then might be a strategy for sending "Message Bearer Teams" from our local ministries? The vision is to see Message Bearer Teams consisting of 3-8 individuals and families leaving their home city and local ministry and purposefully settling among an adopted unreached or unengaged people group. These teams work to see church planting movements (CPMs) developed through implementing Discovery Bible Studies (DBS) through a person of peace. These movements are developed along family lines and close networks of friends. Discovery Bible Studies are a primary tool used among unreached and unengaged people groups to initiate church planting movements. These studies consider central passages in the Bible in a culturally relevant way while also trusting the Holy Spirit to touch hearts through a demonstration of the Spirit and power. In time, these small group studies turn into simple house churches, reproducing through starting further Discovery Bible Studies.

1. Before the Message Bearer Team has been finalized, the local ministry is faithful to wait on God, the Holy Spirit, and allow Him to "set apart" the individuals and families He is thrusting forth. This process is confirmed through God speaking to and leading the individuals and families. These individuals and families undergo specialized training in both the Word of God and how to apply it, adjusting to cultural differences, contextualizing the Gospel and utilizing platforms among the unreached. This specialized training does not necessarily mean traditional Bible school or seminary. Instead, it includes training focused on deepening the Message Bearer in encountering God through His Word and becoming more alive to God and filled with the Holy Spirit. These are the qualities proven most necessary among the unreached.

2. Before being sent out, the individuals and families making up the Message Bearer Team have proven faith and biblical character as well as skills, professions, abilities and spiritual gifts suited for the unreached. The depth of their spiritual lives and their ministry capacity has been proven in the local ministry. They are neither spiritual novices nor simply those wanting an adventure. They must possess a long-term view of their participation in cross-cultural mission. Serving unreached people groups can require a significant period of time to be effective. Members of Message Bearer Teams need a long-term orientation. Before leaving for the field, the team should consider how their skills could practically benefit the unreached people group among whom they intend to live. Once the team arrives on the field, they must be flexible in how their ideas for a "platform" are practically worked out in a particular context.

3. A helpful strategy is to send the new Message Bearer Team initially to a regional center (usually a large city) in the nation or among the people group to which they are called. Here, they learn language and culture well and a strong "central church" is developed. They might remain there for 1-2 years. Then, 2-3 individuals and families can springboard from this regional center to the specific location where they are led by the Spirit. Such a situation is often referred to as a "Launch Team."

4. The Message Bearer Team prayerfully considers a particular "platform" they will implement to serve the community. They find something that is seen by the local people as a felt need that truly serves them. A clinic, hygiene center, training in agriculture, digging water wells, teaching English, literacy or a host of other creative options are possibilities. A platform builds trust among the local people and serves them, providing genuine opportunities to see them opened to the Gospel the team is there to proclaim.

5. The Message Bearer Team develops a nucleus for a self-supporting community of faith in the new town or city. Some have jobs or professions in the new community while others work with their hands to provide forms of sustenance for the

team. As a team, they are a spiritual community or "church" in that new community. Therefore, they are the starting point of the coming church planting movement. They are committed to the four marks of a spiritual community from Acts 2:42 (considered earlier in this section).

6. These Message Bearer Teams are not reproducing a denominational church nor an expression of "church" their home culture understands among the unreached. Instead, they reproduce a culturally relevant expression (to the unreached people) of a community of faith. It is crucial to the sustainability and spiritual vibrancy of the new small group churches that the Message Bearer Teams drop the trappings of their own understanding of "church." Instead, churches are developed along the line of biblical characteristics alone.

IV. Key Principles in Sending

Above, we have considered the end goal of Message Bearer Teams along with some specific and practical ways to select, train and send out these teams from local ministries. Now, let's look at some key principles to follow in the Great Commission Ministry to keep it focused and consistently moving in a "sending" direction:

1. Many more Holy Spirit-filled, God-ordained Message Bearer Teams are necessary to propel the body of Christ toward the fulfillment of Jesus' commission. What if each of our local ministries was sending out 10% of the members of our local ministries in Message Bearer Team to the unreached? If God asks us as individuals to give a minimum of 10% of our financial increase to Him, doesn't it seem fitting for local ministries to consider "scattering" at least 10% of our "best and brightest" to the unreached as well?

2. This immediately raises a concern among leaders about finances. Remember, we are talking about Message Bearer Teams walking out the key principle of becoming self-sustained communities of faith over the long haul through professions, working with their hands, raising crops, etc. However, it is important for Great Commission Ministries to help Message Bearer Teams

initially through six months to one year of financial support from the local ministry. This enables them to get into the local context, learn the basics of culture and language, while prayerfully determining how to become self-sustained.

3. A key principle is for Great Commission Ministries to prayerfully adopt five unreached/unengaged people groups. These five are highlighted among the local ministry often throughout the year. They are a prayer focus of Global Prayer Teams and can be a focus of giving among the local ministry members as well. It is these five that are made the primary focus where the concepts being considered during Mission Forums are discussed and made practical.

It is also surrounding these five people groups that vision is cast for families and individuals to sign the Go Declaration as Message Bearers. The adopted unreached and unengaged people groups should include two in an unreached region of one's own nation (though a different culture than the local ministry's) as well as three people groups in a neighboring or other nation.

Chapter IV.
EQUIPPING MESSAGE BEARERS AND MESSAGE BEARER TEAMS

Steps for Effective Preparation

The equipping of Message Bearers and Message Bearer Teams in local ministries is of the utmost importance. It is often thought that if we love Jesus and others, it is enough to see great fruit among the unreached. Sadly, this has not proven to be accurate. There are specific areas of equipping and training that are necessary for disciples to be made into faithful message bearers in the work of the Great Commission on the front lines.

This section of the handbook concerns itself with some of these equipping and training issues. Much of such equipping will need to be done in an individual way (e.g. reading particular books) while some of it can be done as a "Message Bearer Team" together prepares for serving among the unreached.

Every potential Message Bearer and member of a preparing Message Bearer Team should be strongly considering these suggestions and actively participating in many of them. Historical and contemporary experience across the body of Christ suggests these points of equipping are necessary for effectively thriving as well as producing great fruit for the Kingdom of God among the unreached. These are not necessarily in a particular order.

1. The Message Bearer Team should ideally participate together in a specialized training program for Message Bearers. Such specialized training does not necessarily mean traditional Bible School or Seminary. Instead, it focuses on deepening the Message Bearer in encountering God through His Word and becoming more alive to God and filled with the Holy Spirit on a daily basis. These are the qualities that prove most necessary

among the unreached. Many sending organizations in various parts of the world offer such training, while many other such parachurch groups do as well. This training needs to take into in-depth account at least the following items:

» In depth experiential knowledge of the Word of God and how to apply it

» Adjusting to cultural differences in a healthy way and awareness of the accompanying phases of culture stress and shock

» Understanding and knowing how to apply the concepts of contextualizing or deculturizing

» How to utilize "platforms" among the unreached and through them develop a financially sustainable community of faith among the team

» Implementing non-negotiable habits of successful Message Bearers over the long haul

2. Consistently remind yourself that the orchestrator or director of cross-cultural mission and the Great Commission is the Holy Spirit. He is moving your Message Bearer Team toward the Gospel among unreached people of a very different worldview than your own. He is fully invested in every aspect of what needs to happen to see spiritual breakthrough among the people group being targeted. We need a fresh empowering of the Spirit to reap a fresh harvest among the nations.

» Read the short book *Engaging the Holy Spirit: Understanding His Dynamics in the Great Commission.* This book provides a background on the Person of the Holy Spirit and how He works in and through believers to fulfill the Great Commission. The book reveals the Spirit's functions and roles in the Great Commission and the central concept of being consistently filled with the Holy Spirit as His Message Bearers among the unreached.

3. Read the following three books that lay out basic church planting movement principles and understanding:

» Contagious Disciple Making: Leading Others on a Journey of Discovery

» What Jesus Started: Joining the Movement, Changing the World

» Church Planting Movements: How God Is Redeeming a Lost World

Don't just read them, however. Take notes on them. Consider them together as a Message Bearer Team. Pray about them together.

4. Seek to become as familiar as possible with the culture of the people you will be serving. Learn how they view time, how they view family and relationships, and much more. It is crucial to grow in contextualizing the Gospel so that the people you are reaching can understand it in a culturally relevant way. This has been an area of many mistakes in the past and why more people groups have not been reached with the Gospel.

» A helpful book every Message Bearer and Team should read is *Ministering Cross-Culturally: An Incarnational Model For Interpersonal Relationships*.

5. Learn all you can about the majority religion among the people. It is very important to incarnate the Gospel among the people. One way to do this is through grasping their worldview. Don't seek to change their worldview toward yours but instead communicate the Gospel according to their worldview. There are great "bridges" to the Gospel in every one of the major world religions. Sometimes these are called "Redemptive Analogies" - some practice or understanding, embedded in a culture which can be used to demonstrate the Gospel. To discern them, we need to become knowledgeable in what their religion teaches, what their holy books say, what their culture deems important, etc.

6. Place a high value on the idea that the Holy Spirit seeks to prepare, send and sustain the highest spiritual quality men and women in the nations. This includes the depth of spiritual life in Christ as well as moral excellence, mental acuity, emotional stability and relational skills. Make an effort to be consistently growing in each of these areas. Allow a deep work of God to prepare you for serving among the unreached.

» Read the book *Spiritual Equipping for Mission: Thriving as God's Message Bearers.* This book brings emphasis to the depth of the spiritual life of the Message Bearer and team. Ten spiritual keys are considered that are central to Message Bearers thriving spiritually in their ministries among the unreached. It is the spiritual life and its increasing growth and maturity that allows for the production of the greatest amount of fruit among the unreached.

7. Recognize that one of the greatest attacks of the enemy upon the Message Bearer Team is breakdowns in interpersonal relationships. Determine as a team to openly and honestly, with humility, deal with conflict. Don't let relationship problems linger and seek to avoid the petty offenses we often inadvertently commit toward each other. Keep short accounts and verbally forgive each time another hurts you. Part of the reason for such conflicts is the presence of pride, self-seeking and ambition in every disciple and message bearer. Such realities are often hidden in our hearts. It only takes a teammate or someone working with us to see resentment, bitterness, jealousy and criticism to come to the surface. Though we say we are working for God, just put us in a situation where our ideas, plans and ministry agendas are threatened and watch how quickly resentment and self-pity arise. God allows (and even orchestrates) team situations that are challenging to mold us. Maybe there is an unseen area of sharpness in our personality that continually hurts others. Often, this is tied to a conscious or unconscious pride and self-seeking. God allows someone to work alongside us who rubs against that point and helps make us aware and begin to change that tendency.

8. Learn from others about how to use your university degree or professional skills for self-supporting purposes among the people and location you are going to serve. Spend much time seeking God for wisdom and understanding about how to do this most effectively.

9. Increase your diet of studying the Word and receiving spiritual revelation from the Lord. Devote attention to crucial passages for Message Bearers as you disciple new believers, specifically

the Sermon on the Mount: Matthew 5-7 to prepare for teaching new disciples how to live in the Kingdom and Romans 3-8 to grasp the foundations of our faith and how to reproduce these core aspects among the unreached/unengaged.

10. Determine to evaluate your motives, ambitions and priorities on a regular basis. Guard against not merely serving God or the people group you are going to serve among. Instead, God is most interested in our paying close attention to growing in deep fellowship with His own heart.

At face value, it appears heroic and noble to concentrate our energies primarily on service and activity for God. We buy into the notion that we He cares mostly about is our work for Him. Outward service seems so selfless. Through our devotion to growing in deep fellowship with Him, He is able to overcome our naturally cold hearts toward Him while also breaking down our naturally proud, unbroken natures. It is quite possible to serve God with much Christian activity and yet never have our coldness of heart dealt with nor our proud, self-centered heart touched.

So much of our Christian activity seeks to provide an answer to others needs which few of those who are providing the answers, are actually walking out. Often, a sense of pride pushes us onward to expand our ministry spheres instead of prioritizing seeing and experiencing God in our individual lives and allowing all else to flow from this place. Unless experiencing God is happening we have little to give to anyone in the nations. It is God who wants to touch, transform and restore peoples' lives. Of course, He uses us in this process. However, we must allow Him to move in and through us, without our getting in the way.

Go definitely wants us serving Him among the unreached. But He desires this service to spring from the fountain of a life saturated in knowing Him, seeing Him and enjoying Him in the depths of our being. For many, cross cultural ministry has become an end in itself. When this is the case and we feel threatened we will respond and fight with all our might to protect ourselves and our activities. Instead, the Lord invites us to submit to the circumstance God has allowed and even orchestrated for our own good. Admitting our shortcomings and repenting for our wrong priority on ministry itself, we return to the Lord with a heart and are brought into a deeper experience of God's grace along with His power to satisfy our hearts. It is through a disciple who is being satisfied along with Jesus, that His power will be released and manifest among the unreached.

I. Preparing Ourselves Biblically

A primary area of equipping for Message Bearers and Teams is growing in our capacity to deeply study the Bible and rightly understand, interpret and apply it. We are not only referring to having a right Bible Study method but more importantly the believer themselves being right in their approach to the Word.

Many seek to pass on a particular Bible study method to others with little results. What happened? The method may have been right but the person was not yet prepared to glean all God desired from His Word. Attention must be paid to preparing ourselves to become the largest receptacle of what the Holy Spirit intends to pour in.

The Bible is a spiritual book. It is not made up of mere words but is Spirit. We relate with God (who is Spirit) through our own spirit being energized through Him. We cannot worship Him correctly with only our mind, will or emotions, but in the Spirit. It is the same with engaging God's Word. Since His words are Spirit they must be read, meditated upon, interpreted and applied in the Spirit. This is only done through a human spirit which has been regenerated by the Holy Spirit. But even a regenerated human spirit needs to learn to read the Bible in the Holy Spirit.

Many believers know the general contents of the Bible yet have never spiritually understood it. This is not surprising. They were not yet using their regenerated spirit to grasp and understand the Bible, which is Spirit. The Bible often goes spiritually misunderstood for years for many believers. Why? We have sought to understand with our natural minds instead of receiving revelation from the Holy Spirit. We must become "spiritual" people to receive the "spiritual" Word of God, not relying on natural wisdom.

Every regenerated believer has the Holy Spirit but is not necessarily walking and living according to that Spirit in their lives. It is the combination of having the Spirit plus yielding to the Spirit which prepares us for studying the Bible in the spirit as a "spiritual" person. To believers who are "spiritual," revelation from the Bible is limitless.

Just as the unreached that God is sending us to will not understand the Bible through human wisdom, intellectual knowledge cannot give us spiritual understanding into Scripture. The New Testament regularly refers to "carnality" as a hindrance to a deeper grasping of Scripture. "Carnality" refers to believers who have the Spirit (are born again and regenerated) yet choose not to live under the rule of the Holy Spirit. This does not mean they have no understanding of the spiritual depth of Scripture. But they are only scratching the surface of Scriptural revelation (drinking milk). Milk symbolizes introductory revelation and spiritual understanding while meat represents higher, wider and deeper revelation related to spiritually discerning the Word of God. A vast percentage of believers appear content with spiritual milk rather than meat. What is the cause? Carnality! (or walking after the flesh instead of the Spirit) They have the Spirit but are not yielded and submitted to His rule in their lives. They find it difficult and even foreign to receive direct revelation from God. To effectively grow and teach others from the Bible, a believer and message bearer must be spiritual, ruled by the Spirit of God, willing to die to walking after the flesh.

A subsequent reason behind limited spiritual understanding, wisdom and revelation gleaned by disciples through God's Word is lack of wholehearted surrender to obey God. All believers have access to the same Bible. Why is the light each grasps of such varied measure? Because each person is different in their inner life. Some are open to God, receiving spiritual understanding, while others read but without a willingness to necessarily obey. We see the importance of being open to God in willingness to obey what we spiritually discern. Without it, we find it difficult to rightly glean all God intends through His Word. When there is an area where a believer is withholding obedience, they will dance around the subject in God's Word, avoiding it and not grasping the light God desires for them.

God calls us to approach relationship with Him and meditating on His Word with a single eye. This refers to the need to yield ourselves to the Lord alone. We refuse to serve another. Our surrender to Him prepares us to obey Him. There is no other way to faithfully approach Bible study then this. Apart from complete surrender to Jesus, the revelation and spiritual understanding grasped in God's Word will be limited. We may understand superficial ideas but will not be able to discern the deeper meanings and ideas of the Word. The double-minded cannot glean God's purposes in His Word. We must possess a single eye; submitted and surrendered to obey what we find in His Word.

To study Scripture well requires laying ourselves down in obedience. The degree we are laid down in obedience is the measure of the revelation of His Word God will release to us. It is costly to be a disciple ready to receive revelation from His Word. God may need to bring us through trials and tests in order to do so. We want to be a people paying the price to receive the treasures waiting to be mined. Consistent obedience reveals more clarity to His Word. Following Jesus means willingness to do His will. Some consistently ask what the Bible is teaching. Instead they should ask, "Am I willing to obey His revealed will in every circumstance?" If our response is right, God will always open His Word to us. Failure to grasp consistently deeper spiritual understanding of God's ways reveals a defect in surrender to God.

We find additional principles as we seek to grow as discerning students of the Word of God. Each of these principles are to be developing within us through daily habits and discipline. A hindrance to grasping deeper spiritual revelation is a tendency to be subjective – to allow my own experience to color what is read. Instead, those growing in spiritual understanding approach it with objectivity – allowing it to reveal what it has to say. When we read God's Word our thoughts, emotions, ideas and assumptions need to be yielded to God. We are ready to hear God speak and expect Him to do so.

The notion of possessing growing passion and hunger for God is another important principle. Those who study God's Word want to see God, know God and hear God. Their hunger is consistently being provoked by drawing near to God's presence. This deep desire is crucial to unlocking many of the mysteries of God's Word. We do not merely seek to be faithful in service to God but want God Himself!

It is God alone we are after in His Word. Not His blessings and benefits. A third important principle is that true students of God's Word cannot be careless. His Word is to be handled with the utmost respect. Those prone to carelessness don't learn the deep lessons of His Word.

To be casual with the Word is a travesty. The Bible is exact and purposeful with every word and phrase. Nothing is haphazard in the Bible. We want to seek accurate understanding in the heart of God of why each and every verse is found in Scripture.

To rightly understand the intent of the Holy Spirit in the Bible it is helpful to consider some items. Until we are disciplined by the Lord to enter into these and other principles, we will find it challenging to penetrate the veil of superficiality which often hangs over our study of the Bible.

First, we need to enter into the heart and thoughts of God and what He intended and meant. We want to discern the original purpose of each passage we read. We are not necessarily seeking interpretation but the specific reason why this portion was added to the Bible in the first place. The Holy Spirit has a particular purpose for each passage and we are to enter into that purpose and align ourselves with it. We are following Him as He guides us into deep understanding of Scripture.

Second, we want to align with the Spirit of Scripture. Behind the words, there is Spirit. Much of the Bible is reiterating various facts or doctrines. Sometimes these portions or books get overlooked. There is much Spirit that is meant to be discerned in each of these passages. This reveals what the Spirit intends to communicate through the facts stated. For each of these, the primary issue is not about which method we use to study God's Word, but of our willing to allow the Holy Spirit to lead and have His way in us as we study.

**GLOBAL
MISSION
MOBILIZATION
INITIATIVE**

*" The Lausanne Committee for World Evangelization enthusiastically
affirms the work and vision of GMMI. GMMI's commitment to
mobilizing & equipping the global church toward its role in the task of
reaching the world for Christ is compelling and strategic."*

GlobalMMI.net / info@GlobalMMI.net

>>> **Who We Are:** We are a growing global mission mobilization
initiative multiplying national mission mobilization
movements mobilizing and equipping local ministries
and disciples at every level of the body of Christ.

>>> **What We Do:** We multiply local ministries and disciples for
the Great Commission in three primary ways:
1. An international step by step strategy multiplying
mission mobilization movements at every ministry
level across a national church.
2. A Great Commission Equipping Center (GCEC) in
Chiang Mai, Thailand
3. A publishing arm, IGNITE Media, producing high
quality mission mobilization and equipping materials
and resources.

>>> **Core Objectives:**
1. Movements of individual disciples mobilized and
equipped for Jesus' Great Commission
2. Movements of individual local ministries mobilized
and equipped for Jesus' Great Commission.
3. Movements of individual denominations and church
organizations mobilized and equipped for Jesus' Great
Commission.
4. Movements of national evangelical alliances and
associations in every nation mobilized and equipped for
Jesus' Great Commission,

Other Resources
From IGNITE Media

IGNITE Media is the publishing arm of GMMI. Books, booklets, bible studies, DVD's, blogs and more are produced to serve your ministry in deepening the spiritual life and mobilizing and equipping for cross-cultural missions.
Visit http://www.GlobalMMI.net/resources/

Cultivating Abandoned Devotion To Jesus

God is calling His people into deeper relationship with Himself. This is the beginning of all effective ministry and the only way effective ministry is continuously sustained. We cultivate this wholeheartedness through studying His Word deeply while applying all we are learning. These Bible studies go deep into the heart of God's Word, revealing depths and insight that will revolutionize your spiritual life. These can be used individually or in a group setting.

- Studies in the Life of Joseph
- Studies in the Book of Jonah
- Studies in the Book of Colossians
- Studies in the Sermon on the Mount
- Studies in Jesus' Parables of
  the Kingdom (Matthew)
- Studies in the Seven Churches of
  Revelation
- Studies in Matthew 24 - 25 Jesus'
  End-Times Discourse

Mobilizing Local Ministries

The Holy Spirit is raising a vision of not merely one by one mission mobilization, but the concept of mobilizing and equipping whole local ministries for Jesus' Great Commission. These resources enable that process through the use of proven tools and teaching. Each of these resources serve a unique purpose toward seeing disciples mobilized and equipped through local ministries to serve the unreached.

- Handbook for Great
  Commission Ministries (English,
  Spanish, French, Chinese (both
  simplified and traditional), Thai)
- Great Commission Bible Studies
- Global Prayer Teams
- Six Roles in the Great Commission
- Developing a Sending Strategy
- Wakingthe Giant
- Where's Your Haystack DVD

Equipping For Global Harvest

To see the literal fulfillment of the Great Commission we need to be
equipped in particular areas often not discussed or emphasized. These
resources provide focus on core areas of equipping the Holy Spirit is
emphasizing and that need to be carefully grasped and integrated into our
lives if we will be effective.

- Engaging the Holy Spirit
- Declare His Glory Among the
  Nations
- Proclaiming the Kingdom
- Spiritual Equipping For Mission
- Deeper